q̓weq̓wcy̓ ia naʔl sneena

by

Corinne Yvonne Derickson

B.F.A., The University of British Columbia, 2015

A Thesis Submitted in Partial Fulfillment of
The Requirements for the Degree of

Master of Fine Arts
(Interdisciplinary Studies)

The College of Graduate Studies

The University of British Columbia
Okanagan

November, 2018

@Corinne Yvonne Derickson, 2018

The following individuals certify that they have read, and recommend to the College of Graduate Studies for acceptance, a thesis/dissertation entitled:

q̓weq̓wcy̓ ia na l sneena

submitted by   Corinne Derickson   in partial fulfillment of requirements of

the degree of   Master of Fine Arts/ Interdisciplinary Studies

Dr Virginie Magnant: Faculty of Creative and Critical Studies

Supervisor

Dr Gregory Younging: Faculty of Indigenous Studies

Co-Supervisor

Dr Allison Hargreaves: Faculty of Creative and Critical Studies

Supervisory Committee Member

Dr Christine Schreyer: Faculty of Creative and Critical Studies

Supervisory Committee Member

Dr Margo Tamez: Faculty of Indigenous Studies

University Examiner

2

Acknowledgements

Limlimt to the faculty, staff, and my fellow students at the UBC, who have supported and inspired my work.

Limlimt to my Graduate Committee:

Dr. Virginie Magnat, Dr. Gregory Younging (Co-Supervisors), Dr. Allison Hargreaves and Dr. Christine Schreyer (Supervising Committee Members).

Limlimt to my Community of Westbank First Nation for their moral and financial support.

Limlimt to my whole extended family living here and abroad

Limlimt kukuxst to my parents, children and grandchildren for the amazing support and sacrifice

Limlimt kukusxt to my ancestors (Grandparents) for the *captikwəł*.

Dedication

Dedicated: In Memory of Mourning Dove,

to my Children and Grandchildren as the future generations of storytellers to remember

The importance of the *captikʷaɬ*.

Always believe in the strength of who you are and where you come from.

In Memory

Dr Gregory Younging

March 18, 1961 – May 3, 2019

Quillandquire.com

Abstract

My research has been based upon the *captikʷəł*, the traditional stories of the *Syilx* people, and more specifically the work of my Great Grandmother Mourning Dove in her book *Coyote Stories, Tales of the Okanagan*. The *captikʷəł* is a traditional form of storytelling. The "storyteller" brought the stories alive through embodiment of the characters, sometimes breaking out into a song or dance. The stories told of a time before human existence, a time characterized by the animal people. The *captikʷəł* (ancestral oral stories), were traditionally told in the *Syilx* language, within the *q'wc'i?* or (*kekuli* in Thompson) is the traditional winter home of the *Syilx* people.

Captikʷəł is a very important form of storytelling that served as a traditional form of education. The stories convey important protocols about life, laws and lessons. The *captikʷəł* I performed, titled *q̓weq̓wcy̓ ia nath sneena* (Chipmunk and Owl Woman), is at the heart of this investigative research exemplified here in script form based upon the original writing and spelling taken from Mourning Dove's book of 1933. I perform this *captikʷəł* in a performance style, modelled by my late Great Grand Uncle Dave Parker. He was a respected Elder of the *Syilx* knowing five languages, the songs, stories and culture of our people. He often spoke in the language and told a story. He would sing a song on the drum followed by singing a contemporary song while playing his guitar, banjo or fiddle. His performance style captivated many of us whom were lucky to be in his presence.

In my art-based, mixed-method research I use Indigenous methodologies working in the four directions on stage. This methodology is also found in other Indigenous artists of theatre like Margo Kane, Floyd Favel or James Luna. I have worked extensively with the four directions, using the medicine wheel, as an art-based Indigenous methodology to reflect my holistic approach as I call upon the energies of the spiritual realm. Using the four directions I incorporate *Syilx* protocol and language to introduce myself. I embody the characters using the *Syilx* language, dance and song. Performing within the sacred architectural spaces built to reflect the *q'wc'i?* (winter home of the Syilx) I bring the audience to a place of a time in history that Mourning Dove describes as "when the world was young" (Dove, *Coyote Tale*s 7).

It is a multilayered, multifaceted exploration that is holistic in practice and touches upon the cultural, spiritual, social, anthropological, environmental, historical and educational. This research of the *captikʷəł* is an embodiment that connects the emotional to the spiritual. It fosters the understanding of and advocates respect and honour for the feminine relationships.

Lay Summary

This creative support paper is based upon the investigative Indigenous Art-Based Research Method practice employing the *Syilx captikʷəɬ* as a storytelling performance. Using the 13 Grandmother moons as a feminine structure to the *enowkinwix* to engage with multiple layers surrounding the specific *captikʷəɬ* "Chipmunk and Owl Woman" by Mourning Dove, published in 1934. Working from a *Sqilw* feminine perspective this support paper reflects the *Syilx* epistemologies like Mourning Dove explains in her book, from when the world was young to contemporary times. It is an exploration of the *captikʷəɬ* and feminine perspective based on this story to exemplify the importance of how oral tradition and storytelling /performance practice had a purpose that is just as important to the present and future generations. The oral transmission of knowledge meanings, translations and affects are explored through this paper.

Figure Table

Glossary

spaqt Jan/Feb All white time

kpuxwəxwtan Feb/March drifting snow

skərniŕ mən March/April buttercup

peckɬtan April/May budding leaves

sṗiƛəmtəm May bitter roots

miktu?tən June Sunflower Seeds

ksiyaya?tən July Saskatoon Berry

xw̌ əyxwaytan July/August Red Thorn Berry

ɬəxǐ axt' ən August chokecherry

skə̓ lwistən September Red Salmon

ska̓ yikstən October/November Dry Fall Leaves

kca̓ ?ca̓ ?ɬtan November/December Cold weather

smuqwəqwtan December/January Snow Fall time

mook mook tk̓ unalx – snow dress ancestral name as spelled in Mourning Dove's book

Quintasket – Mourning Dove's surname – qwən ta̓sq̓ət blue/green sky- dark clouds

Humishuma – Mourning Dove or Hemishmish

Suqunaquinx , Syilx – name of the Okanagan people

sqilxw- the people

captikʷəɬ- the ancestral stories – come from the spark

nsyilxcen - *the language*

limlimt – thank you

Pia – red tailed hawk – place name for Mourning Doveṡ home land

Sta?qwiłnuit – my home land Windy Bay

kiƚ owna – what now is Kelowna

Teequalt- Mourning Doveṡ Grandmother

sneena – Owl Woman
q̇weq̇wcẏ ia - chipmunk
na?l - a similiar expressive word to the english version of *and* (joining to nouns)

e yayaya ta to pa – to refer to sweatlodge

yayȧm tȧ tu̇ ṗa? – sweatlodge song – great grandparent

q'wc'i? winter home

nwixɬn   knowlege
ƚa?xȧn - ladder

snka? ki? iwsx tx̌a x̌a?n cutn – spirit

k̇əɬ pax̌a mintn – mind

sqiltk – body

pu? u̇s – emotion

in na?k̇ʷulamn scmatet – traditional

cawts – behaviour pəx̌n cutn - elders

i? sxʕapana? ca cun tət   na?kʷulamn - customs

suxʷma?maymay?m teachers – n̊ nəqsilt extended family

i? ƚats mi ən cut - Native Self Actualization

i? tx̌a? x̌a? ncut n tət - spiritual

nəqsiɫxʷ - primary family

nk̓cwixtn - tribe

k̓wak̓wuɬstx taks pəx̌pax̌t - education

sən? icknmsəlx - recreation

nunxʷina?tin - religion

ank̓ʷa?k̓ʷul ̓st - social

i? ı̓ cəniɫts miy n cut - Self Actualization

k̓ʷa?k̓ʷuɬst - training

i? l cəniɫts - self

The Four Directions

n?iƛ̓tk - north

swtimtk – south

sk̓lxʷtan – west

sk̓ʷƛptan- east

Table of Contents

13 Moons of Grandmother Council

"There are two things that I am grateful for in my life. The first, I am a born descendant of the genuine Americans; the Indians; the second, that my birth happened in the year 1888"

(Dove, *Coyote Stories* 3).

I am a direct descendant of Mourning Dove with bloodlines of the *Syilx, Colville* and *Sniyxt* tribe. A Maori Scholar Linda Tuhiwai Smith, pointed out in her address to the audience at the 2017 Indigenous Art Intensive that it is not appropriate to ask; 'Who you are?" but to ask "Where are you from?" Interestingly my parents come from similar families that share a common bond related to the thunder. On my Mother's side of the family the name *"Quintasktet "* translates to blue/green or dark clouds whereas on my Father's side of the family *"Chuchuwasket"* translates to thunder clouds. Both families have a connection through these names to the thunder and lightning storms which bring a powerful energy of strength and perseverance. Over the generations my ancestors lived within the territory from the North Okanagan of the lakes, including the Arrow Lakes to the South Okanagan of Osoyoos, and down into the United states to *Pia*. Mourning Dove's father, Joseph *Quintaske*t, was born near what is now Kelowna (Dove, *A Salishan* 4). The place I have been living at for most of my life is on the West side of the lake from (Kelowna) at *Sta?qwiłnui*t translated by my Ancestors as Windy Bay.

I received the name of *mook-mook-t'kunalx* (Snow Dress) by my mother as a gift on my twenty-fifth birthday. This name is the name of Mourning Dove's Mother's Grandmother, who was the wife of Chief *See-whehk-ken* (Dove, *A Salishan* 11). With the honour of a new name I left behind my baby *Syilx* name. My work is based specifically on the *captikʷəł* revitalizing the previous initiatives *of* Mourning Dove – *Hemishmish*; a Great, Great Grandmother according to *Syilx* family protocols. It is an ethnocultural performance, informed by my interdisciplinary research from a *Syilx* feminine based epistemology. This work explores the *captikʷəł* as a traditional form of performance. It honours the past by translating the wisdom into the present in its usefulness for the future. It proves the seven generational theory of Indigenous epistemology.

This paper is structured within the thirteen Grandmother Moons to reflect the council of the Grandmothers together with the cycle of the moon in every month. The moon, like the women, go through a twenty-eight-day cycle. This is defined by Jeannette Armstrong, *Syilx* Scholar in the *Native Creative Process* as "sacred ancient knowledge" (46). I weave a layer of meaning into each moon that can be related to the *captikʷəł* itself. It is an *enowkinwx* style from a *Syilx* Indigenous methodology that relates to the tradition of the *captikʷəł*" (Armstrong, *Syilx Oraliture* 27). The *captikʷəł* is defined as the oral stories and knowledge that have been passed down through generations. Mourning Dove collected and archived these stories and published them in 1934.

Within this *Syilx* structure I look to the Grandmother council to "speak" through the moons of each sections as the matriarch of my extended family. Armstrong shares, "The Grandmothers often hold the positions of power and honour within *Syilx* epistemology" (qtd. in Corrente 50). Within the structure of this creative support paper, in addition to my exhibition and performance, I honour the Grandmothers. To hold a "Grandmother Council" is to be part of one of the highest *Syilx* protocol.

1st. Moon ~ *Spaqt*

Captikʷəł

The *captikʷəł*, for the *Syilx* people, are the ancient stories told in the winter, within the heart of our families, hosted in *q'wc'i?*, the traditional winter home. The storytellers, who served as entertainers as well as the first teachers, were very popular with the children. The stories were not fables, like contemporary stories, but sacred knowledge-based stories that served a purpose.

My Mother Delphine explains here:

> "Within the *captikʷəł* we are taught how to live life, how to care for each other.
>
> *ixi? i? təl captikʷəł ki kʷu ċax̌ʷ stim tac ḱa?kin mi x̌ast i? scxʷəlxʷaltət, tac ḱa?kin mi kʷu ctəxinwixʷ*
>
> ...and how to take care of the *təmxʷula?xʷ* (land) and we are also taught about
>
> *uł tac ḱa?kin t x̌ast stəxistim i? təmʷula?xʷ. uł nixʷ kʷu ċax̌ʷax̌ʷ i? kəl sqi?s, ḱʷulncutən kʷu cuntm i? l sqi?s., ḱʷulncutən*
>
> ....how the Great Spirit will show us answers within our dreams."
>
> (Delphine Derickson, Oral Interview 2018)

My mother, Delphine, told me the *captikʷəł* stories . I enjoyed listening to these stories. She explained that her Grandmother, whom she calls "*Kakna,*" told her the *captikʷəł* stories over and over again. By the age of six my mother recalled that she knew all of the *captikʷəł* stories. The *captikʷəł* was important to learn, she said, as it gave her a clear understanding of who she was as *Syilx*. It also informed her of where *Syilx* land existed. The *captikʷəł* in my mother's time was told to her strictly in the *Syilx* language by her grandmother. By the age of six my mother could recall every place name within the *Syilx* territory. *Kakna* was my mother's favourite story-teller. My mother recalls her Grandmother animating the stories, going into the characters and acting them out. Similarly, Mourning Dove's favourite storyteller, *S'wist-Lane* (Lost Head), also told very animated *captikʷəł* stories. "He would jump and mimic his character, speaking or singing in a strong or weak voice, just as the animal persons were supposed to have done" (Dove, *A Salishan* 10). Storytelling is not only for entertainment but is also used as a holistic traditional education tool. Joanne Archibald, a Stolo Scholar, who also researched oral storytelling discusses this knowledge in her research *Story-work*, "The Elders taught me about seven principles related to using First Nations stories and storytelling for educational purposes, what I term story-work: respect, responsibility, reciprocity, reverence, holism, inter-relatedness, and synergy" (Archibald 9).

Theory is developed with regard to *Syilx captikʷəł* "as a distinct oral artistry possessing a complex layering of meanings" (Armstrong, *Syilx Oraliture* 37). The purpose of the *captikʷəł* stories therefore was to teach. The storyteller transmitted these stories to inter-generations of *Syilx* people. These stories are personal, family, community and tribal histories. We know where we come from due to the stories shared by the storyteller. The stories are layered with symbolic textural images that are described in linguistic *Nsyilxcen* terminology. The stories set the stage for layered symbolic images within the imagination of the listener. To fully understand these metaphors you must have knowledge of the cultural context. In contemporary times these stories have been translated into English for public publishing purposes. However, in the process of translation from the *Nysilxcen* language to English some of the meanings in the story have been lost. Mourning Dove explains that *chip-chap-tiqulk* is the name of the animal people. They are "accounts of what really happened when the world was young" (Dove, *Coyote Stories* 7). To know the full meanings of these stories you must know the language as there are metaphors attached to different *Nysilxcen* words. In my discussion with co-academic graduate student Mariel Belanger most recently, we contemplated the inherent ways our Indigenous thought processes work which follow the patterns of the oral traditions found within the *Nsyilxcen* language that echoes the natural rhythms and patterns of nature which does not follow a western structure. The oral storytellers may at the first visit only give you a piece of the story until the next visit.

My work is the performance of *Syilx* storytelling (the *captikʷəł*). It is an exploration of *Syilx* Indigenous epistemology, that follows my family lineage through Mourning Dove. This creative research process is defined in *Syilx* terms by *Syilx* scholar Jeanette Armstrong, who is a Canada Research Chair in Indigenous Philosophy: "*i? sqelxwlcawtet*, is the fourth order of human existence. It is the spiritual act, which celebrates, enhances and contributes to the first three activities, while pushing out into the unknown" (Armstrong, *Native Creative* 70). It is a performance-based creative exploration that weaves the spiritual, mental, physical and emotional through the act of storytelling. This performance paradigms exists within Indigenous philosophy, education, community and individuality. It empowers the Indigenous right of being on *Syilx* land through the generations.

It is the goal of my research to reawaken and breathe new life into these stories. Influential qualitative inquiry scholar Norman K. Denzin discusses the performances of Indigenous people as it must not follow the historic "Indians playing 'Indian' for white faces" as in the Buffalo Bill performance era. The work must be done for the resurgence and archival purposes of knowledge (Denzin *Indians on Display* 13-31). It is important that our authentic voice as story-tellers is heard. The stories must be told by the people for the people. Telling the stories for the people is an important part of *Syilx* culture. Harry Robinson, a prominent storyteller of the Smilkameen, shared with anthropologist Wendy Wickwire "that the stories would disappear with his disappearance from this earth" (29). The continuance of this traditional storytelling must continue into the future generations through the storyteller. The Sqilw storyteller has a job to do according to *Syilx* ways of being. Robinson told the stories (fulfilling his purpose) to ensure the stories would live on. He hoped future generations would take interest in the stories to become a passionate storyteller as he was and "to live by the stories" (29).

Lastly, the *captikʷəł* is a communal exercise. It does not exist in isolation, as Indigenous epistemology is a holistic practice. It is a shared experience between community, family and new nations only, as it exists within its own indigeneity. Gerald Vizenor, Anishinaabe writer and scholar states, "The invention of the dominant society have nothing to do with the heart of the people" (qtd. in *Writing In Oral 55*). The *captikʷəł* exists at the heart of the people. The *captikʷəł* exists at the heart of the people within communities told by the Elders who were all heart!

2nd Moon ~ *Puxwəxwtan*

Family Stories - Smy'may

> *" Story-telling is an ancient profession, and these stories are among our oldest possessions"*
>
> (Chief Standing Bear qtd. in Dove, *Coyote Stories* 3).

Grandpa's Story

    Smy'may are everyday stories that recount experiences or historical references (Armstrong, *Syilx Oraliture* 103). Grandpa's stories would tell of many oral accounts and family stories as the *smy'may* does. The stories came from generations past. Families are our bridge that connects us to stories that tell of our history and culture. In the past it was not uncommon for an individual to name six generations back of ancestors. It was a big extended family that filled the ears of oral traditions handed down from generation to generation. My Grandfather would say after his initial greeting upon seeing me, "So what do you know…?" I would respond with a newsworthy story that would lead to hours of storytelling. Grandpa's stories told family history of the Okanagan- Colville connection. Silko, a Laguana Pueblo writer, confirms the family stories importance: "The Stories are always bringing us together, keeping this whole together, keeping this family together" (Silko qtd in Veilie 25). Grandpa awakened the spiritual cultural warrior, the protective spirit, to protect our land, our ways of being and most importantly our families. He taught me to be animated through these stories and to "believe." Grandpa's stories were a mixture of *captikʷəł* stories, Indian war time stories, and personal family stories passed down through generations.

When Grandfather shared many the stories with me, Grandma would just nod in approval of his stories with a smile. Other stories were of cultural significance. Grandpa sometimes would say, "I would tell you some stories about coyote, but he wasn't always that good. Sometimes he was bad (a trickster)."

The *smy'may* my Grandfather would tell me, sometimes that included those of family origin, from my Great Grandfather Mickey Derickson. He was a storyteller that contributed to family stories and to a collection of stories "Coyote & the Colville" compiled by the Omak Mission in 1925. My paternal grandfather's family was from the state side of the Okanagan *Syilx* Nation known as *Colville.* Grandpa claimed we had Nez Perce in our family lineage. Chief Joseph was a favourite story my Grandpa would tell. He told me of how Chief Joseph sent warriors ahead to ask for assistance in his tribe's fight against the US Calvary. During Chief Joseph's fight with the US Government, my Great Great Grandfather reported a warrior who was seen at the Nesplem Days gathering. He wore a cavalry jacket that showed his aptitude as a warrior and signified that he killed a US Calvary personnel.

Grandma's Story

Grandma would listen quietly as Grandpa told the stories to me. My grandmother came from a place called White Man's Creek. She would tell me stories of her father and mother, how they worked to survive on the land. Grandfather would sometimes go by canoe across the lake to get groceries. It was a shorter distance by canoe compared to travel by land to Vernon. Grandma shared how her grandfather was a carver. He made two pipes, inlaid with silver and copper, a resource found in the mountains above and mined by his own hands. Grandma kept these pipes in a safe place where we have yet to find them. Grandma would also repeatedly tell me of how her Grandmother, Annie Joseph, remained at the Arrow Lakes. At this time I did not know the significance of this information. Now I know this oral account repeatedly told to me carries a lot of political weight concerning land claims. The family oral stories have proven to be important historical references to the *Syilx* family history. Every story connects the people to the land and its resources within *Syilx* territory.

3rd Moon ~ *Skərniɾ' mən*

Residential School:Resilience

"In the way of the Native Narrative Tradition, it counsels and cautions: Any honourable relationship must be based on honour, dignity, and mutual respect. Any other footing seeds disaster" (Johnson qtd. in Allen *Voice of the Turtle* 21).

Residential Schools were initiated in the year 1884 by the Government of Canada by way of the Indian Act. The Government of Canada, along with the Government of the USA, had a plan to "kill the Indian within the child." It became the law for the children to attend residential schools: LaForme states, "In the 1800'as the Canadian government established a policy to aggressively assimilate Canada's first inhabitants into English speaking Christian Canadians" (qtd. in Degane et al. 54).

The children left the comfort of home, living in multigenerational family structures, to live in an institutional school supervised by Catholics Church of Canada. Left behind were the grandparents who told the stories in the language, as well as Aunts, Uncles, Cousins, Brothers, Sisters, Mom, and Dad. Left behind was the traditional diet of deer, moose, elk roots and berries. Left behind were the traditional medicine ways of the land and the traditional ways of being.

Justice Harry S. Laforme quotes Duncan Campbell Scott (Indian Affairs, 1913-1932): "I want to get rid of the Indian problem. Our objective is to continue until there is not a single Indian in Canada that has not been absorbed" (LaForme qtd. in Degane et al. 54). The children were held in captivity, prison-like darkness. The children were subject to slavery, to starvation, and unthinkable abuse (spiritual, sexual, physical, emotional and psychological). The children could no longer speak the language, sing the songs, or dance. Their long hair was cut short as they tried to cut the cultural ties of their ancestors (54). Because of residential schools the *captikʷəł,* language and all traditional ways of the *Syilx* have been subject to the dangers of extinction. The school attempted to use the bible, with memorized verses, to replace the *captikʷəł* stories. The government had many attempted action plans to erase the traditional ways of being. The Nuns and Priest replaced the storytellers. "Removing the child from the wigwam, superstition and helplessness…Through the terrible example set by their parents, and thus depraved" (55). This was the goal of the Government of Canada. The Canadian government tried in numerous ways to "kill the indian."

My Grandfather's stories of Residential School were horrible. It was hard work for him as he endured laborious long work days outside on the school's farm. He prayed enough times a day on his knees during residential school to make up for the rest of his life, as he would tell me in those words when I would ask him if he wanted to come to church. Residential school, my grandfather shared, taught him how to steal to avoid his hunger. It was a starvation experiment we now know from the truth and reconciliation reports. Grandfather told me how he sometimes ate rotten potatoes just to ease his hunger pains. I was hurt to know of the experiences my Grandfather endured at residential school. What a terrible thing he had to endure.

My Grandmother, Mourning Dove was also institutionalized within a Catholic boarding school in Washington State (Dove, *A Salishan* 26). In Mourning Dove's autobiography she writes how her mother sent her to the mission "obeying Father de Rouge in fall of 1898" (26).

Like many Indigenous people Mourning Dove and others since have regarded the Catholic Religion as a secondary belief. She writes in her autobiography that she would often pray to *ku-lencuten* and to God. My Grandfather on the other hand rejected the Catholic teachings as an adult as he would say, "I prayed enough times down on my knees during residential school to last a lifetime." With the Truth and Reconciliation process many of the churches built upon reservations across our territory remain almost empty. A lot of the Elders that remained loyal to the church have passed on to the spirit world. I take the opinion of Mourning Dove as well praying to *kulenchute*n and to God, whereas I include prayers to Jesus, Mary, Joseph and Buddha at times. Coyote might be of great help too when you really need some power I say (see the *Senklip* trickster moon).

However, regardless of the government's genocidal policies the stories and knowledge survived to be transmitted from my ancient parents to me. In my research I have contemplated this question: Could the *captikʷəł* have foreshadowed the modern day attempts to "kill the indian" (genocide) with symbolic meaning using people-eating monsters (including *Sneena* - Owl Woman).

4th Moon ~ *Peckɬtan*

Mourning Dove: Hemishmish

"I was always a dreamer....At night I would lie awake in the tule-covered tipi and build air castles of future bounty while my tired parents took their well deserved rest" (Dove, *A Salishan* 32).

My Great, Great Grandmother, Mourning Dove, was the first Native American Woman to be published in North America. She was my Great, Great Grandmother's Sister on my mother's maternal side. She did not have any children. However according to extended family protocols of the *Syilx* culture, she would be considered my Grandmother. Traditionally your Grandparents' siblings become your Grandparents as well. It would be disrespectful to call them anything otherwise. Mourning Dove knew the *captikʷəɬ* were so important to record for future generations. In her autobiography she records how she was taught many of the traditional ways by her parents and grandparents within her beloved land, in the Kettle Falls ~ Kelly Hill area of Washington State. The *Suqinaqinx* were living in the traditional ways at this time. The way of life changed drastically for Mourning Dove as she became a pre-adolescent with the coming of the white settlers and government policy. She was forced to live in the missionary school and learn the ways of the colonizer.

In spite of experiencing religion in the Catholic run school Mourning Dove's early traditional puberty training helped her to retain her connection to her culture. She sought to share the *Syilx* ways and stories for future generations. It became a goal for her to compile the stories for publishing. Mourning Dove's determination led her to take a business course where she learned how to type. Working in the orchards back home she typed the stories by oil lamp at night in a tent. By day when she wasn't working in the orchards, she visited the Elders to collect the stories. Mourning Dove would also publish *Coyote Stories and Tales of the Okanagan*. She credits a "blue eyed man" who assisted her in the publishing of her works (12). Chief Standing Bear wrote the following foreword for Mourning Dove's book *Coyote Stories*: "So, in writing the legends of her tribespeople, *Humishuma* is fulfilling a duty to her forefathers, and at the same time she is performing a service to posterity" (6). Mourning Dove credits many of her Elders for the stories as well as an adopted Grandmother, *Kat-atqhu*. She would spend hours listening to her stories after riding down to her tipi on her buckskin horse to visit: "I used to love to have the old lady hold me in her withered arms and tell me stories and history" (Dove, *A Salishan* 95). My Mother often refers to the *sqilw* as "shadows of each other" a translation to one of the words to describe us in *nsyilxcen*. I have come to understand this in more depth as I have grown older. Science itself is catching up to this knowledge that the experiences that live in our DNA through our blood memory affects our present day experiences. Therefore, in my research I credit Mourning Dove's life and my blood lineage. Over the last few years I have felt close to Mourning Dove through doing this work. More so with this experience. In confirmation of the work I do to revive these stories, I had the following experience:

One day I was searching the book shelves in a shop in Northern BC. I happened to be looking at scientific and mathematical books while thinking of my late Uncle who had passed away. I walked along another row of books and turned the corner. When I turned the corner, I looked directly back and up to the top shelf where I saw this older looking book. It was Mourning Dove's publication of *Coyote Stories* dated 1934. It was in perfect condition. I was amazed. I immediately had to have it. So I bought it to bring it home to show my family what prize I had acquired.

This day I believed I was led to my Grandmother's book, to continue her work. I had just finished my undergraduate degree by developing workshops for youth entitled *Captikʷəł* Theatre. Coincidently I was drawn to the work of Augusto Boal's *Theatre of The Oppressed* inspired by Paulo Freire's *Pedagogy of the Oppressed*. Oppression seemed to be the common thread between the work of my *Grandmother* and the work of these *Grandfathers* of performance theatre.

I am thankful for that day. It was a confirmation for me, from the spirit world, that I was on the right path. I continued to do the work of my Grandmother Mourning Dove in a new way into my graduate work. In between my degrees I attended a "Mourning Dove Symposium" put together by scholars in the USA that have studied her work and life. It was then that my family was informed of the treatment Mourning Dove had endured, including her sterilization without consent. This was an act of genocide carried out by the US Government with statutory force. This violent non-permissive procedure purposely set out to hinder and destroy Mourning Dove's future lineage by interrupting the Indigenous transmission of knowledge, a deplorable act experienced by many that goes down in history as shameful and against human rights. However, the government did not take into account Mourning Dove's extended family lineage. Here I am as a living testimony to my ancestors continuing the work to transmit her work to future generations.

5th Moon ~ Spiƛ̓əmtəm

Captikʷəɬ - q̓weq̓wcy̓ ia nath sneena

Chipmunk and Owl Woman based on the original story by Mourning Dove
Coyote Stories 1934.

I include this *captikʷəɬ* in script form here to repeat the story in my performance and to reiterate the importance of the *captikʷəɬ* itself. It is placed here in the fifth moon within the very heart like the siya berry of the Grandmother's 13 Moons.

Characters: *q̓weq̓wcy̓ ia* - Chipmunk - a lil girl, lives with her Grandmother

(kot se we ah - Mourning Dove's spelling)

stimteema - Grandmother Rabbit lives with her Granddaughter

sneena - Owl Woman - a ruthless feared hunter of children

wy-wetz'-kula - Meadowlark - the tattler and gossip

Chipmunk & Grandmother were going about their day

Grandmother (Stimteema) ~ *Calls to Chipmunk:* Come here Granddaughter.

Chipmunk (q̓weq̓wcy̓ ia) ~ Yes, Grandmother?

Grandmother ~ I am going to make some soup for lunch

16

How about you go pick some *siya* berries for us and I will make some *siya* mush for dessert.

Chipmunk ~ Ok!

Grandmother ~ Just be sure to go pick some berries quickly at our picking place and come right

back. You know there are dangers to watch out for in the forest.

Chipmunk ~ Yes Grandmother I will go and pick some berries at my favourite place. Don't

worry Grandmother I will be back soon. See you.

Chipmunk ~ *Sings as she is walking thru the forest.*

"I am a little Indian girl" ~ *Goes to her berry bush.*

Chipmunk ~ *Picking berries.* - One berry ripe. Two berries ripe. Three berries ripe…

She stops to listen as she hears footsteps under the bush.

Owl Woman (Sneena) appears with a big basket with many children on her back.

Owl Woman ~ *Kot se we ah*, your father wants you!

Chipmunk ~ I have no father.

Owl Woman pauses to think for a moment.

Owl Woman ~ Your Mother wants you! She wants you to come home.

Chipmunk ~ My Mother died many snows ago. *Chipmunk laughs making a chattering chipmunk sounds.*

Owl Woman ~ Your Aunt wants you to come home.

Chipmunk ~ I never had an Aunt. *Chipmunk laughs again with making chattering chipmunk sounds.*

Owl Woman ~ Your Uncle Wants you!

Chipmunk ~ That is funny. I never had an Uncle!

Owl Woman ~ Well, *Owl Woman sighs.* Your Grandfather wants you!

Chipmunk ~ That is strange; my Grandfather died before I was born.

Owl Woman ~ Your Grandmother wants you to come home right away.

Chipmunk ~ *Thinks silently for a few minutes and says to herself ~ If Grandmother wants me to come home right away I better do as she says. She turns to Owl Woma*n ~ I will not come down unless you hide your eyes.

Owl Woman ~ All right. I will hide my eyes. See! I have them covered. *Owl Woman pretends to hide her eyes placing her clawed hands over them, leaving spaces where she can see.*

Chipmunk ~ I can see your big eyes blinking behind your fingers. I shall not come down until you have hidden them entirely.

Owl Woman ~ Ok. I will this time. *She hides her eyes again. Leaving a little crack to see through.*

Chipmunk really thinks that Owl Woman's eyes are covered. Not taking any chances of being fooled, Chipmunk jumps from branch to branch to the ground from the top of the bush. She jumps clear over the top of Owl Woman's head and as she goes sailing over, Owl-Woman reaches for her. Owl-Woman's fingers claw down Chipmunk's back, ripping off long strips of fur, although the little girls gets away. Ever since that time the chipmunks have carried the marks of Owl Woman's claws; the marks are the stripes you see on the chipmunk's back. Chipmunk runs and runs and Owl Woman followed as fast as she can.

Chipmunk ~ *Trembling and out of breat*h. Sneena! Sneena! ("Owl - Owl!")

Grandmother ~ What is wrong grand-daughter …Did you step on a thorn?

Chipmunk ~ *Sneena! Sneena*! *Chipmunk keeps repeating in a frightened voice.*

Grandmother ~ Oh …*dath dooth!* (A *Syilx* expression). Come hide in my bed.

Chipmunk cannot keep still; she runs around under the robes.

Grandmother ~ Here, hide in my berry basket. *She places her in the berry basket.*

Chipmunk is making too much noise.

Grandmother ~ Hmm... Ok, here, hide in my pot of soup!

Chipmunk almost drowns. She and Grandmother are in despair.

Grandmother ~ Oh my! Oh I am sorry. What will I do with you Chipmunk. You are not

cooperating. It is hard to hide you without you being found. What do we do? Owl

Woman   will soon be here.

Then enters Meadowlark (Wy-wetz'-kula) singing :

"Two Little oyster shells,

Hide her in!"

(repeat x1)

Grandmother ~ Come here granddaughter …Hurry!

Grandmother ~ hides chipmunk between the two oyster shells and, knowing Meadow Lark is a gossip and a tattler, she takes off her necklace and throws it to the singer (as payment).

Grandmother ~ Here take this and do not sing a word Meadowlark. This is one of my best bone necklaces made by my handsome husband years ago. He is gone now so please take it and be quiet. Owl Woman is coming.

Owl Woman - Hoo Hooum! Hoo Hooum!. Where is the child that I am hunting?

Grandmother ~ *Grandmother pretends she does not know. Shaking her head.* I don't know. I sent her to pick berries for me before the sun was high.

Owl Woman ~ Where is she? I smell a chipmunk.

Owl woman looks under the robes on the bed, in the berry basket and in the soup. She looks everywhere she can think of. At last she almost gives up and turns to leave when she sees meadowlark the tattler flying back to the tree near the teepee lodge.

Meadowlark ～ I will tell you, if you pay me.

　　I will tell you, if you pay me.

　　Where she is. Where she is!

Owl Woman hurries outside and throws a bright yellow vest to the Tattler, who puts it on and

　　sings

Meadowlark ~ Two little oyster shells

　　Take her out!

　　Two little oyster shells,

　　Take her out!

Then Meadowlark flies away, dancing and showing off his new necklace and vest.

The necklace she was given for helping Chipmunk and the yellow vest she earned for tattling she

　　wears to this day.

Owl Woman ~ *Pushing Grandmother.* Out of my way you old woman... Hoo Hooum!

Owl Woman ~ *snatches chipmunk out of the oyster shells. With her sharp fingers she cuts out*

　　chipmunks heart and swallows it.

Owl Woman ~ Eh Yom-yom! It is good. Little girls' hearts are the best! *Owl Woman walks away*

with the basket of children on her back smacking her lips.

Grandmother ~ *While crying over top of her Granddaughter, she hears a familiar voice.*

Meadowlark ~ *Singing*   Put a berry in her heart!

Put a berry in her heart!

Grandmother ~ *Dries her tears, then Grandmother puts a half ripe Siya berry in Chipmunk's*

breast and sews up the hole. Then Grandmother steps over chipmunk three times.

Chipmunk ~ *takes a deep breath and jumps up screeching.*

Chipmunk and Grandmother ~ embrace...in delight and relief......

This story reveals how Chipmunk got her stripes, and how Meadowlark got his yellow vest and black necklace. It models the important relationship between Grandmother and Granddaughter. It depicts the Grandmother's role as the first teacher, disciplinarian and support. It emphasizes the importance of Grandmother's wisdom. It warns of possible danger from the "hunters" of children symbolized by Owl Woman – *Sneena*. It has an important relationship to present day issues concerning women, especially missing and murdered women, as well as past issues of governmental genocidal crimes against the Syilx. This story teaches us that we must turn back to the wisdom of the Grandmothers to promote the healing necessary to move forward as Indigenous people, which is why this thesis is written within this structure of the 13 Grandmother Moons.

6th Moon ~ *Miktu?tən*

The Trickster - Coyote

"Trickster is a doing not a being" (Archibald 6).

Coyote or *Senklip* is the trickster in the Syilx *captik^wəł* stories. In many stories he is the main character. Coyote demands attention in his frequent role as trickster. On a serious note, *"Senklip* was given a purpose to help the Spirit Chief in preparation for coming of the people to be humans (*ku sqilxw*)" (Robinson 33). He wanted desperately to have an important name, so he tried to stay awake all night. He wanted to be the first one to Spirit Chief's lodge, as the first one to his lodge could have first choice over all the names. However his plan failed, as he fell asleep even though his eyes lids were held open by sticks. He was unresponsive to the animal peoples' greetings as they passed by on their way to Spirit Chief's lodge. To their amusement they realized *Senklip* was not awake at all but actually sleeping with his eyes open. By the time *Senklip* made it to the Chief's lodge the sun was high in the sky and all the important names *Senklip* wanted were already taken.

Through *Senklip*'s trickster ways we learn what not to do or sometimes what we can do. He gets into mischief and sometimes causes big trouble. He has special powers where he can shape shift into another being, which actually gets him out of trouble a few times. In life and death situations *Senklip*'s power comes to the rescue. Spirit Chief also gives him a special brother fox with powers to bring *Senklip* back to life, should he happen to be killed (Dove, *Coyote Tales* 7). Coyote, as a trickster, is intelligent, cunning and transformative. He is funny and makes us laugh in some of the things he does in the story. He is sometimes a hero as well, fulfilling the role of getting rid of the *people-eating monsters*.

In the stories my grandfather told, he would not share with me some stories about *Senklip,* as *Senklip* would at times behave immorally being sexually inappropriate. Later in life I would learn these stories from my Mother, or Aunt, where it was more appropriate to share according to *Syilx* culture. Coyote is an archetype that is given special powers, as the story is told by many Elders. However, within the story we all (as *Syilx*) have the potential to find ourselves sharing characteristics with Coyote. The Elders say that Coyote is our ancestor or ancient parent: "Coyote is after all one of our ancestors as transmitted by Harry Robinson in his creation story of the twins" (Robinson 10).

Coyote makes an appearance in my *captikʷəł* performance of "Chipmunk and Owl Woman." When he emerges from around one of the log pillars, he is laughing as he enters - as usual. He challenges Meadowlark to a *stick game*, as a quest to try and win Meadowlark's new vest and necklace. Meadowlark was just showing off his new attire challenging the handsome looks of S*enklip*. How dare he challenge *Senklip* for this position, as *Senklip* believes he is the most handsome. *Senklip* makes a brief appearance, which gives the audience some comic relief right before Owl Woman's final act, when she cuts open the chest of Chipmunk. As Armstrong writes, "Coyote's travels across the land are a record of the natural laws of our people learned in order to survive"(Armstrong, *We Get Our Living* 1).

7th. Moon ~ Ksiyaya?tən

The Transmission of Oral Knowledge

I Sing*

I am a Little Ndn Girl

My Home Is Everywhere

I Wander Thru the Lonely Woods

And Never Seem to Care

They Tell me it is Wrong

To Ride My Life Away

But What Bit do I Care

For What They Say

The Forest is My Home

And There I am going to Roam!

For I am a Little Ndn Girl!

*A song my mother taught me in childhood. I decided to spell Ndn in this way as to mimic my Mother's accent. Importantly, we are not "indians" as Christopher Columbus named us. We are *Sqilw* or *Syilx* or *Sukinaqin* (see glossary).

I remember watching my Mother's every move as she beat the drum, listening intently to the songs she sang as I felt my heart synergies with the rhythmic beat of the drum; I thought: I too will become a singer one day!

Songs are part of the *captikʷəɬ*. The songs are inherent knowledge. I am a *Syilx* singer. The songs choose me. To sing is to be a keeper of the songs. My acts are continuance links. Armstrong discusses this transmission of knowledge as the process by which "consciousness continues and knowledge continues unfolding from one generation to the next" (Armstrong, *The Native Creative* Process 82). The songs are sacred and alive. Within the songs lives a power of past generations and knowledge embedded in the lands, the trees, the birds and the wind.

Music is a creative inquiry methodology of Indigenous arts-based research. From its ancient uses in the *captikʷəɬ* to more recent methodologies in music it is a process that deeply touches parts of the soul. Music is social, historical and medicinal. *Syilx* music and songs have been used in ways of healing and ceremony for generations. Music is medicine that spans through centuries, time and space. As noted by ethnomusicologist Catherine Grant, "the inextricable link between music and other forms of intangible cultural heritage means that a loss of musical heritage may have wider repercussions for cultural vitality at large: it may also mean the loss of the unique language contained in song, for example, or of related theatre or dance forms" (48). I use song and sound in my performance practice, as would the original storytellers of the *captikʷəɬ* (Dove, *A Salishan*158). For example, Meadowlark has a specific sound that is indigenized using *Syilx* sounds from the language, and I mimic this sound in my performance. I learned these sounds from my Mother as we performed this story together with our family with puppets.

Indigenous performance artist Peter Morin says this to support the inclusion of Indigenous languages within the arts: "It is imperative to include language within the constructs of Indigenous arts and performance where possible" (Morin 32). Language is an important link to our Indigenous culture ways, therefore it must be in the process of our creative acts, as emphasized by Morin: "The language is a creative act, just like any other creative act. When you are speaking your language, you are making something. your speaking becomes a small contribution to the survival of your community" (32).

I am a semi-fluent speaker, so I feel it is my duty to transfer this knowledge to the next generations ensuring it survives. The use of *Syilx* language within the arts allows for "authenticity and linguistic *Syilx* pedagogy" (Armstrong, *Syilx Oraliture* 74-79). The language is a vital resource that I am committed to use and to preserve. For example, I use the *Nysilxcen* names of the characters in the story when I performed "Chipmunk and Owl Woman." I also gave the audience a lesson in the *Syilx* language at the beginning to allow them to connect on a new level of *Syilx* education. During the story telling performance process, I would frequently alternate between the characters and the narrator. This technique of the *captikʷəl* storytelling is a long tradition going back to the idea of shapeshifting, therefore I shape-shift or transform into the different characters of the story to give the audience an experience of this historic technique. I shape-shift the audience to a historic time and place. As the audience becomes immersed within the story in this way, time and space transcend into a different dimension inside the architectural space of the *q'wc'i? (Makwala's Kekuli.)*

Armstrong writes, "With the loss and endangerment of our language through colonization, it is most important to implement or use nysilxcen wherever possible" (Armstrong, *Syilx Oraliture* 46). Currently, Okanagan worldview, knowledge, culture and people are facing extinction. Bill Cohen, a *Sqilw* Indigenous scholar, also states: "It is up to all of us to reconnect to those strands of knowledge and create new systems that balance creativity and survival" (Cohen 4). As a *Syilx, Sqilw* or *Sukinaqin* (all words to describe who we are) Woman, it does not matter so much as the work does, I am looking forward to further creative art works using the language. I feel it is also my duty as the women before me in my family lineage to archive and transmit this knowledge for future generation. Using the language within my work is an important goal. I agree with Morin as he writes: "It is our duty to the young people to revive and learn the language fluently, and to the knowledge base, even if we are learners" (Morin 34).

8th Moon ~ X̌ʷ əyxwaytan

Sacred relationship - Granddaughter and Grandmother

My Ancient Parent

Grandmother who hit the drum with reverence taught me the song

Grandmother whose song I remember in the sweat house

Grandmother who held me when I was scared

Grandmother who wrote the stories

Grandmother who picked the berries

Grandmother who rode the horses

Grandmother who taught me the language

Grandmother who disciplined me

Grandmother who laughed with me

Grandmother who visited me in my dream

I Honour You

"I called my grandmother by the baby name of Patee. When she arrived, she took me into her lap, smoothed my tangled hair and crooned" (Dove, *A Salishan* 8).

In *Syilx* culture the Grandmother and Granddaughter relationships are very important. We read about it in Mourning Dove's autobiography (Dove 8). It is discussed within many Indigenous forms of literature. I chose Mourning Dove's story "Chipmunk and Owl Woman" from Coyote Stories 1934 to illustrate this relationship for a few important reasons:

a)   Within the story, the main characters are Grandmother Rabbit and Granddaughter Chipmunk. It is a symbolic display of the sacred relationship between Granddaughter and Grandmother. It is one that I myself hold so valuable in my life. My Grandmother was like a Mother to me. I spent a lot of time with my Grandmother even as an adult.

b)   I also had very many adopted Grandmothers as a part of my life, each one leaving me with a special gift.

c)   Many children were raised by their Grandmothers, sustaining the traditional forms of language, songs, craftwork, food and medicine. Children were taught by their Grandmothers to look after oneself, the family and community. The knowledge is passed down from generation to generation (Dove, *A Salishan* 10, 16, 40).

d)   This is a sacred relationship with a sacred trust. When we get back to these forms of traditional ways of being then we will be closer to healing the earth. These traditional forms being respect for the girls, women, mothers, and especially Grandmothers. This relationship to the Grandmother to hold her in high regard is thus of great importance to the *Syilx*. Armstrong writes: "It took a long time for me to realize the value of having a Grandmother who could speak to me in the total purity of the words which have been handed down through thousands of years, from mind to mind, from mouth to mouth" (qtd. in Corrente 50).

Within the *captikʷəł* shared by our Elders, we are taught to respect the land. Everything that is given to the *Syilx* people to sustain our lives comes from *tmxulawxw* - meaning Mother, and *xwulaw*, meaning the land. We always give thanks to *tmxulawxw*, (our provider, caregiver our Mother) (Joseph 92, 145). My Mother Delphine describes this notion as, "We get our living, like milk, from the land" (quoted in Armstrong, *Native Creative* 2). The land is compared to our Matriarch, Mother or Grandmother we gives us nourishment and life. My Great Grand Uncle Dave Parker defines this same notion in the *Syilx* language as *Tumtumtet* ~ the Mother: "It is from her breast we suckle to get nourishment" (a metaphor for the land and resources). This was expressed in Uncle Dave's oral speech at *Komasket*, as he translated the words and meaning of the Okanagan Nation Declaration of 1984.

Therefore, we learn the value of sacred relationship between the Mother, the Grand-mother, the woman, and the girl, the feminine power. When these relationships are valued again, society may begin to heal. The crimes against all feminine power are directly related to the crimes against mother earth. It is the restoration of the balance between the male and female which will bring hope for the future generations living again in harmony with the Mother: "The children are taught at a very young age to be connected to the land through using all of their senses" (Joseph 26-29). We belong to the land instead of the land belonging to us. "They never say how for the Indians to belong to what they have claimed," says Harry Robinson in *Living by Stories*, written in the exact way he spoke (Robinson 9). He meant to explain the *Syilx* teaching of how the people belong to the land, not vice versa.

I structured this text according to the *Thirteen Grandmother Moons* to represent the ma-triarchs of the thirteen Grandmother council. The Grandmothers were the matriarchs of the family. They often had a lot of influence in major decisions as they still do today. Armstrong dedicates her whole book of Poems Breath Tracks to her Grandmothers: "In memory of those Okanagan Grandmothers whose blood and words live inside me"(qtd. in Lutz 112). Additionally the thirteen moons make up a full year as we travel around the four seasons. This is an important process to take along with the Grandmothers as it is a part of the *Syilx* protocols to observe the whole year of thirteen moons as a transitionary collective of time, knowledge and action before moving on to something new.

9th Moon ~ ɬəxǐ axtʼən

Sacred Woman

"I knew who the powerful people in my family were, and they were women"

(Armstrong qtd. in Corrente 50).

Woman

Women are sacred

Living, Giving, Nurturing from the very breast of life on Mother Earth

The circle of woman

Celebrating, Living and Being

The woman

One blood

One soul

multigenerations.

Armstrong defines the Syilx tribe as an "egalitarian society" (qtd. in Corrente 159-160). However, being a female artist, my work comes from this feminine perspective. The woman being connected to this important cosmology of the moon with the feminine cycle of menstruation, prepare to give life or give the undeveloped cycle of life back to mother earth. The connection between woman and earth is a sacred revelation to sustainability and a renewal of life in the most holistic sense: "Pre-contact American Indian women valued their role as vitalizers, because they understood that bearing, like bleeding, was a transformative act... The blood of woman was, in and of itself, infused with the power of the Supreme Mind" (Allen *Sacred Hoop* 28). The moon time of a woman was a very powerful time supported by being in sync or ceremony during this time. The woman was connected to all of the universe. Women were said to be *xaxa* (meaning sacred) at this time.

Women have been over the generations connected to sacred ways of being through plant or spiritual knowledge which have the ability to heal; Andy Joseph and Mourning Dove both confirm that the medicine, as found in the act of Grandmother in the story "Chipmunk and Owl Woman," is "sacred knowledge held by the Grandmothers" (Joseph 34, Dove, *A Salishan* 45, 68). In her autobiography Mourning Dove describes how she seeks healing by her women relatives north of the Canadian border (near Osoyoos). She writes about seeking healing from her sister; there she would be treated and healed by the women folk in her family. The women in her family knew the ways of healing with herbs (Dove, *A Salishan* 79, 202). Women are connected to the higher levels of knowledge through generations. Ann Cameron, a Canadian writer, states: "The wisdom of the woman must always be kept sacred, just like the very blood of woman itself. There will come a time when there will be great changes. This is the time where the act of knowing and the act of doing will be very important" (Cameron 52-53).

This is the sacred healing power of women, the relationships to each other and to the land. It is always giving and strong. Douglas Cardinal speaks of "soft power" as "resilient, giving, flexible and strong" (32). The women of the *Syilx* are strong and powerful women inherently. We know from our family history of our Grandmothers living to be well over one hundred years of age and riding horseback into that age as well. The women of the *Syilx* were also visionary leaders relied upon by their families and communities for direction. Women were also

"Chieftains in some of the Okanagan villages, whom were called *Skumalt,* women of great authority" (Armstrong, *We Get Our Living* 12).

Many Indigenous women are making waves in the Indigenous academic work. Most describe it as a "duty" to community. It is about the survival of Indigenous culture. Women are able to give birth, so have the ability to create, transform and transcend. As Allen writes, "Women were capable of all ritual magic, as they had the ability to bring new life into the world" (Allen 28). With the invention of feminine hygiene products, we no longer have to be confined to the menstrual huts. The taboos and protocols of the past are now in question. Women are evolving and leading the Indigenous evolution in academia. Is it because women have the heart? Looking back to the story of Chipmunk and Owl Woman, Grandmother replaced a Saskatoon berry where Chipmunk's heart was before Owl Woman ripped it out. This is an important lesson and message to the women of *Syilx* lineage. The *Syilx* women are sacred vessels being the "givers of life" and knowledge.

Additionally we learn the spiritual and healing connection from Grandmother who sews chipmunks chest back together with sinew replacing her heart with a soya berry, while singing her song. It is another clue to the knowledge that the Grandmother's inherently hold. I trace my lineage from my ancient parent of 1888, the time of my Great, Great Grandmother Mourning Dove, to now the photograph exhibit I created as part of my research, I have either photographed one of these strong *Syilx* women of my lineage or included a photo from the past. A photo exhibit' that I will continue to update to honour the seven generations of Grandmothers (see photos in the appendix). I end this section of my thesis with a quote of Mourning Dove's Mother

Lucy speaking to Joseph her father on the subject of her spiritual training: "Women are known to make good doctors. We need them every bit as much as warriors" (Dove, *A Salishan* 45).

10th. Moon ~ *Skə́ lwistən*

Sacred Architecture

"In the past Native Aboriginals of North America lived their lives in harmony with nature and their own nature. It was a way of thinking, a way of being.It was not a way of adversary, of being adversarial to nature and one's own nature."(Cardinal 5).

My people imitated the sacred architecture of the rocks, the land, the earth, the stars, the planets, the sun, the moon and the universal systems that exist beyond. Housed in a womb underground, the *captikʷəɬ w*as told and retold for generations in the *q'wc'i?* (winter home). Traditionally we followed the sacred knowledge of our ancestors to build our structures within the sacred architect of the circle. Living in this way we stay in harmony and balance with mother nature. We become part of the sacred architect aligning our bodies, minds and spirit with the universe. Lee Maracle, a Coast Salish Author, discusses the generations of mothers: "In the centre stands my Mother, her Mother, her Mother's Mother - infinite lines of Grandmothers, who spiral out and gain numbers and accumulate strength in their numbers" (qtd. in Corrente 140). The oral stories Maracle describes are "traditional tribal narratives that possess a circular structure incorporating event within event, piling meaning upon meaning until the accretion finally results in a story" (qtd. in Corrente 34).

Within the story ~ look for the circle ~ travel throughout the spiral ~ try not to hit the ground ~ elevate to a place of sacred knowledge ~ a place that existed generations before ~ connected by the quest for creative knowledge.

Kateri Damm quotes Campbell who describes the Indigenous concepts of time and history: "In this telling: History is not linear, chronological and progressive, it is a spiral in which there is no clear beginning, or end. It is a web in which people and action and are interconnected" (Campbell qtd. in Dame 101). It is this spiral that connects time space and family lineage. Finding where you are on the spiral is an act of liberation from the mindset of this colonial time. Similarly, in the *Native Creative Process* Armstrong defines the word "*Sqilxw*" (the *Syilx* word for ourselves) "as to dream in a spiral" (Armstrong, *Native Creative* 111). Therefore, our lives are essentially a sacred architectural dream dimension. We are a living architectural design. In my own dream I am an Eagle Dancer, like the eagle I fly (dance) soaring with the winds creating and reaching out into the far unknown.

Figure 1. Cori-dancing in Dole France - Swiss Alps in the Distance 2015.

Cardinal compares the flight of the Eagle with the creative dream state that opens onto visionary experiences: "Like an Eagle, you fly out there on your own abilities. You swing and soar with the breezes and float higher and farther. You move for one point to another, aware and totally alive, comfortable to be out there past the edge of the known realm, into what is only possible" (Cardinal 85).

See figure 2 below. I chart the artistic dream architectural journey within the *q'wc'i?* (*Syilx* Winter Home) to attain the highest goal of creative self-actualization. The *Nysilxcen* words were sourced by my Mother Delphine Derickson.

Figure 2.

Q'wc'i? Nwixɬn – **Winter Home Knowledge**

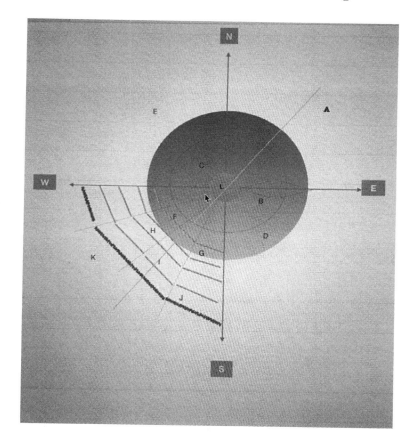

Figure 2 ~ Legend

A.   ɬa?xản - ladder

B.   snka? ki? iwsx tx̌a x̌a?n cutn – spirit

kə́ɫ pax̌a mintn – mind

sqiltk – body

pu? u̇s – emotion

C.   in na?k̓ʷulamn scmatet – traditional

cawts – behaviour pə́x̌n cutn - elders

D.   i? sxʕapana? ca cun tət   na?k̓ʷulamn - customs

suxʷma?maymay?m   teachers – n̓ nəqsilt extended family

E.   i? ɫats mi ən cut - Native Self Actualization

F.   i? txa? x̌a? ncut n tət - spiritual

nəqsiɫxʷ - primary family

G.   nk̓ cwixtn - tribe

H.   kwak̓wuɫstx taks pə́x̌pax̌t - education

I.   sən? icknmsəlx - recreation

J.   nunxʷina?tin - religion

ank̓ʷa?k̓ʷul ̓st - social

K.   i? l̓ cəniɫts miy n cut - Self Actualization

k̓ʷa?k̓ʷuɫst - training

L.   i? l cəniɫts - self

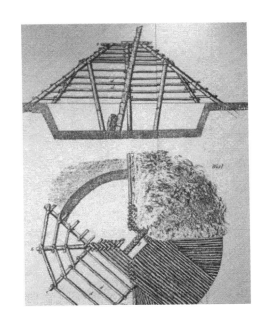

Figure.3 Syilx Winter home
Easton 177

The Four Directions

n?iʎ́tk - north ~ swtimtk - south

sklxʷtan - west ~ sk̓ʷʎptan - east

Figure 4. Enowkin- 1st Performance Venue

Figure 5. Makwala's Kekuli 2nd performance venue

11th. Moon ~ *Skȧ yikstən*

Syilx Pedagogy:Performed Body Movements

My research to embody the performative storytelling of the *captik*ʷəɬ led me back to the pre-puberty training system of the *Syilx*. It is fascinating to explore *Syilx* Indigenous forms of movement, as it applies to the traditional teachings. Armstrong describes the Okanagan phrase, "*i? sqelxwlcawt* - refers to how we train as individuals within our culture, as a deliberate part of our existence" (Armstrong, *Native Creative* 14). In this way of *Syilx* traditional teachings we learn disciplined body movements that lead to physical fitness accustomed to the *Syilx* lifestyle. Living in harmony on the land we have created a body memory that is very attuned and holistic. Snowber relates this practice in his words, "Notable scholars described the lived experience of the body as central to knowledge and learning, and early curriculum theorists had huge influence through incorporating the lived experience into their scholarship, paving the way for dancers and movers, to continue to theorize and embody their way of inquiry" (Snowber, qtd. in Leavy *Handbook of Arts* 252). The Indigenous body and Indigenous movements are unique to the people, dating back centuries, to living on the land. The specialized movements are reflected by the *Syilx* pedagogy of living in harmony with the land and being one (Joseph 95). The importance of embodied ways of knowing is also discussed by Snowber, who envisions "the body intelligence as grounded in the senses and impulse and gestures of the body as a place of inquiry" (252-3).

The breath plays an important role in this embodied inquiry as it is also the case in Japanese cultural practices, for example in Tai Chi. The role of the breath is the very essence of life itself. Learning to control the breath in different situations became a normal way of being to *Syilx* people as they often travelled along way over rough terrain, while hunting and swimming across a lake divide, or running up a hill. Sometimes learning to breathe quietly, or not to breathe at all for a period, was used in survival purposes. The control and use of breath in these circumstances come from the oral traditions of knowledge passed down from Elders to youth, to ensure survival and good health (Dove, *A Salishan* 40). The breath plays a big part in the holistic movement of Indigeneity. In breath and in repeated movement and ritual of ceremony, our body works holistically. Secrets of Indigenous pedagogy may be deemed a "ceremony, ritual or performance" (Luna 14). James Luna, a Californian Indigenous performance artist suggests that performance may be an "opportunity to express traditional culture without compromise" (14). Within my Indigenous performance work my objective is for my whole being to work together, body, mind, emotion, breath and spirit to achieve an ecstatic performance as when I Eagle Dance. I embody the eagle using the four elements I dance. This dance connects me to the sacred architectural dream as I fly spiralling and creating with every step.

The *Syilx* people have specialized movements to control the body in a traditional way. The body is used as a tool, or important vessel to move from point A to point B. People were trained to carry out unique feats during puberty, to train in the traditional way of the *Syilx*.(Dove, *A Salishan*. 34-48). The movements, I believe, reside in the genetic make-up of the *Syilx* body memory. This is very advantageous to me as a *Syilx* performance artist. For many *Syilx,* these movements were carried out in our lineage by our parents or Grandparents. For example, my mother was taught in this strict *Syilx* manner. Snowber suggests that, "No word can completely proclaim what the body deeply knows" (247). I recount the training my Mother taught me: "Do not walk like an elephant or drag your feet," she would say. I was taught to walk delicately and with poise. I had to walk with my head up not down. I was trained to be aware of my body. I had to be aware of where I placed my feet. This was the training of walking on the land: centuries old movements, specific to a culture and used for a specific purpose. While in conversations with Tomson Highway and Floyd Favel, each shared with me knowledge of universal Indigenous body movements connected to the land. It was as simple as kneeling or sitting on the land. These repetitive movements in action and relationship to the land it inevitably connect the holistic being (physical, mental, emotional and spiritual).

In my own work I have been developing exercises that are Indigenous-based. I have created a theatre exercise that combines the honouring of the four directions with the yoga-based salutation of the sun exercise. I have made it a life long journey to honour the four directions using the medicine wheel inspired by teacher/Elder Phil Lane, Sioux knowledge keeper (Lane 35). Phil Lane has been a spiritual advisor, knowledge keeper and writer, publishing a collection of handbooks on healing, cultural knowledge and spirituality in the Four Worlds Project. The book Sacred Tree published in 1989 with its 3rd edition has been one of my favourite reference book. It is an amazing experience to combine the Indigenous methodologies with contemporary performance decolonizing spaces in a liberation act. Performance to me is an opportunity to be, when I dance or sing or tell a story it is a direct act of resistance to the past colonial oppression that existed. In contemporary times we may be able to practice who we are although as a Nation of Indigenous People we have lost so much. For those of us who have been gifted with a family lineage of knowledge keepers it is our peoples' responsibility to share and showcase the pride of who we are as Indigenous people. I show this pride as a performance artist as I believe, like Augusto Boal and Paulo Feirre, that through the arts you can attempt to change or influence the masses by expressing your political agenda by creating and performing art, engaging with people. This is what the secret influence to the oral storytellers traditional job was (to engage with the people). With mainstream society sitting behind screens the time now is now is critically important to re-engage in the traditions of personal engagement to listen to a story, practice listening and communicating. It is up to us as Indigenous artists to find ways to revive, revitalize and reconcile these ways of being through storytelling, performance or art.

12th. Moon ~ *Kcả ?cả ?łtan*

Inspiration:Dedication

"Authenticity is not a goal for Indian people, but a prison." (Luna 28)

It is not the amount of time you spend with someone. It is how they change your life.

(Inspired by my time spent with James Luna.)

James Luna, a performance artist of Payomkawichum, Ipi and Mexican-American origin who is best known for his "artifact piece," presented his introductory work at UBC's Okanagan campus during the Indigenous Art Intensive, on July 5, 2017. I attended his performance workshop on July 9-11th, 2017. During his July 12th performance I watched in amazement his unusual but familiar performance — familiar because he reminded me of the great ones (past Elders) from my nation. His use of uncanny or unorthodox actions, like spraying a bottle of air freshener into the audience, or lighting a makeshift pipe in ceremony on stage, or imitating an ancient mask that he shows on the projection screen results in a montage of interesting but confusing Indigenous performance acts. Much like the trickster known to Indigenous people, Luna blurs the stiff protocols of our Indigenous culture. It is abnormal to light a pipe made out of plumbers construction pipe to use in ceremony on stage. No, the Elders would not like that, but here is a performance by Luna poking fun at the seriousness of Indigenous protocols. Humour is indeed traditional to the Indigenous people: we understand laughter and teasing as it is part of our culture. I couldn't help but giggle and wonder "What the hell is this guy doing?" He pushes the boundaries of what is or what isn't real according to the audiences. He seeks to provoke non-Indigenous people/settlers by making fun of their stereotypes they have created about Indigenous culture. W. Richard West Jr, Founding Director of the National Museum of the American Indian, describes the work of Luna: "As you approach the work of James Luna, please check your platitudes at the door and leave your clichés behind. Luna is the unexpected" (qtd. in Luna 7). Paul Smith, a Smithsonian Curator at the National Museum of American Indians asks: "Was it really a pipe, or was it just a mash of pieces put together to resemble a pipe? Was it ceremony, or just art? Luna's work celebrates Indigeneity, but also challenges it" (qtd. in Luna 29, 38).

James challenged me during the workshop when he critiqued my performance. It was a challenge I would take up in my Interdisciplinary MFA Performance. In Act Two of my performance, I jump out of the traditional music genre and into country music style, by singing four songs dedicated to James and inspired by my past family teachers who were also musical (Uncle Dave Parker, as well as my Grandfathers on both sides of the family). Luna mentioned Patsy Cline, thus I sang "Your Cheating Heart," "I Fall to Pieces" and "Storms Never Last" (Waylon & Jessie). The final song was "Go Rest High on the Mountain" by Vince Gill. I dedicated this song to James Luna because he lived on the mountain top.

Smith shared this about James: "Like many of our Elders, James lived high on a mountain top upon the La Jolla Reservation" (qtd. in Luna 46). Many of our Elders loved the mountains like Luna who lived on the mountain top, where you have the clear skies at night with a good view of the vast stars in the sky. It is a past time of mine to stare at the stars at night. The stars are a very important source of being to the Indigenous people. My Grandfather spoke of using the stars as navigating your way in the wilderness. Also the Elders know from the stories that this is where our spirits come from when we are born and the path we take when our spirits go back through the stars. Smith describes Luna's home, "On clear nights, ancient starlight washes over Palmar Mountain, and he can see forever" (46). The Elders also say when one passes it is not death but it is only a transfer of worlds. I was very saddened to hear of James transferring into the spirit world. Smith wrote: "James Luna known as one of the most dangerous Indigenous artists alive; an escape artist and was compared to a super hero, now passed into the spirit world, March 4, 2018" (46). "Most dangerous," Smith writes, because James Luna challenged the racism, the oppression and even the Indigenous status quo through his art. He performed a life time of engaging the audience into thinking about the questions he bought forth through his actions. Many people offered condolences on his Facebook page, as I also did by sharing my commitment to carrying on the work he challenged and inspired me to do.

Final words for this moon written in a true spirit inspired by the trickster into this section like Luna just in case you were confused by his reference to a "prison of authenticity" in the first quote. I understand this concept as a warning that we can fall into the trap of only playing the "indian" as stated by Denzin, in "Indians on Display." It is important to provide historical context and cultural protocol. You must provide reference to Indigenous authentic art which I believe is anything we create in the spirit of our culture (as Indigenous artists). It is up to us as the Indigenous artists to push this envelope. Luna's advice to the contemporary artist is "to mount a serious challenge to the accepted order of things involving indians, a prerequisite for making Indian conceptual art" (28).

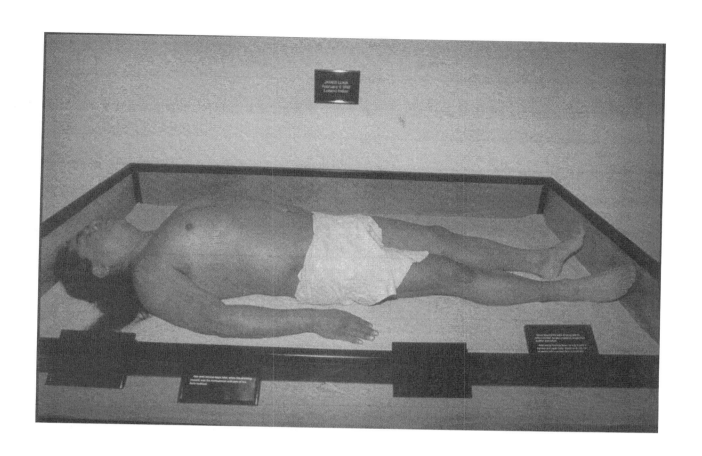

Figure 6. - James Luna

THE ARTIFACT PIECE, 1987 & 1991

13th. Moon ~ Smuqwəqwtan

End of the Grandmother Moon Cycle

In the conclusion of my thesis, I end with these thoughts concerning art and performance, as we are Indigenous artists, we make and create art from our experience and knowledge. We are the thru lines that connect ourselves to our ancestors. We are that mark on the spiral of the dream. We create art from our inquiry, from our curiosity, and from the deepest parts of our soul. Hawaiian scholar Manulani Aluli-Meyer contends that seeking knowledge entails using all of our senses as it is a "cultural sensory/act" (60). It is imperative to tell our stories and to continue to create our art forms using our Indigenous ways. Globalization has opened the door to easier travel, networking and sharing. Being exposed to different cultures within my travels has influenced my art practice. When we travel and experience other cultures we grow and expand our knowledge holistically. Therefore, as we expand our knowledge we expand our work.

It is a priority of the highest order to restore the *captikʷəl* and the *Syilx* language. Once, everything was spoken in our language, as was the *captikʷəl*. Armstrong writes: "Through our true language we can further the purpose and essence of our meaning" (Armstrong, *Syilx Orali-ture* 46). *Syilx* Indigenous people must look back to these ancient forms of knowledge informed by the *captikʷəl* to assist our ways of being and to understand the world around us (Armstrong 46). Our people had this ability to see what we now need to remember. It is important to continue to tell our stories and continue to do the research in our own ways, as to benefit community and not only the academy (Meyer 146-7). It is yet to be seen what creative practice we artists engage in to tell our stories in the future.

Indigenous artists and scholars know the benefits of our transmission of knowledge into artistic practice. Holistically Indigenous artistic practice of all mediums is necessary to preserve an ancient way of knowing. The research must continue, for as Cree scholar Greg Younging states, "The aboriginal voice contains valuable paradigms, teachings and information that can benefit all of the World Family of Nations" (qtd. in Armstrong *Looking at Words* 179). Performance of the *captikʷəl* is a research initiative that can be compared to performative social science research, the fusion of social science and performance. Social structures and elements that can be defined within the *captikʷəl* important to contribute knowledge to modern Indigenous and non-Indigenous societies. It can inform and educate in a meaningful and restorative way.

Additionally, after being introduced to Patricia Leavy's publications as an Indigenous scholar who engages in Art-Based Research I think it is imperative as important to continue the uniqueness of creating interdisciplinary artistic ways, to cross boundaries, to explore theoretical, epistemological, and methodological innovations, and to create a new performance paradigm that is Indigenous-based (*Methods Meet Art* 175). There is so much work to do within the Indigenous performance arts to push the boundaries while creating a way of being to preserve our Indigenous cultures within the work of the creative arts.

Denzin states: "As researchers - qualitative researchers of all traditions - we are uniquely equipped to take up this charge, to reach beyond the walls of the profession, to engage with disparate and competing publics, effects, if not changes, the course of the historical present. That is the charge of this volume of work. We have a job to do. Let's get to it" (*Q. I. Past, Present & Future* 462). This particular job I take seriously, to plot the course on this journey connecting past research on the *captikʷəɬ* by my Grandmother and applying it to modern day understanding, to bring context to my artistic endeavours. As Denzin also writes, "The new trends move from academic to interdisciplinary scholarship, expanding and refining qualitative art-based research and performance ethnography" (*Q.I.Neoliberal Time*s 1-13). This trend is good news for me as I continue to research and create interdisciplinary ways of using Indigenous methodologies. I define my work as ethnocultural performance, interdisciplinary art-based practice grounded in culture and Indigenous feminine epistemology. It is a multilayered, multifaceted exploration that is holistic in practice and touches upon the cultural, spiritual, social, anthropological, environmental, historical and educational. This research of the *captikʷəɬ* is an embodiment that connects the emotional to the spiritual. It fosters the understanding of and advocates respect and honour for the feminine relationships.

Further exploration of the *captikʷəɬ* in the original language must be undertaken to restore the higher knowledge and understanding. The *captikʷəɬ* must be given its original role in *Syilx* society. Stories can contribute to transforming society. The *captikʷəɬ*, like Augusto Boal's Theatre of the Oppressed, has the ability to be consciousness-raising, and to impact public and policy research concerning health, mental, emotional and social structures. It is empowering, educational and entertaining. To revitalize ancient art forms like storytelling by transforming them in new ways through performance, for example, opens up creative possibilities. It is ethnocultural, ethno-cinema, and intercultural arts education. *Captikʷəɬ*, as a performance exploration, can be a worthwhile ongoing research to fill and reconcile cultural voids.

Within the end of this cycle of *13 Grandmother Moons*, another cycle begins: I will continue my practice, while I encourage other artists and scholars to continue dreaming while creating within the spiral. Sometimes the dream finds you, as in a dream one night about 20 years ago, when I saw my *Stimteema* (who died when my Mother was 6 years old). She was sitting there waiting for me it seemed at my Mother's home but she was not alone. Her and the Grandmothers were all lined up sitting in the way we describe as the "Grandmothers' Council" wearing their skirts and handkerchiefs on their heads. This is why I wanted to honour and remember the Grandmothers. *Puta? ntmi? Anxa? cantata*

Appendix A

Figure 7. Seven generations of lineage, from Mourning Dove photos above - below buffalo skull as Mourning Dove was deeply affected by seeing the round up and killing of Buffalo in Montana; stumps carved with characters of the *captikʷəɬ* chipmunk and owl woman with Syilx names inscribed.

Figure 8. Mourning Dove- McWhorter Collection

Figure 9. Painted Portrait Mourning Dove

Figure 10. Mourning Dove - photo

Figure 10. Mourning Dove -
McWhorter Collection

Figure 11. Women's baskets and deer hide dress sculpture

Figure 12. Grandmother tule sculpture

Figure 13.
Performance in the *Kekuli* with Grizzly Bear
Standing - Representing Chief Standing Bear

Figure 14. Aunt Hazel and I

Figure 15. My Mother Delphine
Derrickson performing early
80's.

Works Cited

Aboriginal Healing Foundation. *Reconciliation & The Way Forward. Edited by Degane et al.,* Government of Canada, 2014.

Allen, Paula Gunn. *The Sacred Hoop: Recovering the Feminine American Indian Tradition.* Beacon Press, 1992.

Allen, Paula Gunn. *Voice of the Turtle: American Indian Literature -1900-1970.* Ballantine Books, 1994.

Archibald, Joanne. *Indigenous Storywork.* UBC Press, 2008.

Armstrong, Jeannette C., *Syilx Okanagan Oraliture and Tmixw Centrism. U of Greifswal,* 2009.

Armstrong, Jeanette. C. et al. *We Get Our Living Like Milk From the Land.* Theytus Books, 1994.

Armstrong, Jeannette C. in Lutz.Harmot, *Approaches to First Nations Cultures;A Collection of Essays on Native American and First Nations Literatures and Cultures.* U of Greifswals, 1999. pp.171-187.

- - - *Isole Nella Corrente Tribalsimo E Ricerca Dell' Identitita' Nella Cultura Dei Nativi Canadesi.* Messina, Italy:U of Messina, 1992-93, pp.12-78.

- - - and Douglas Cardinal, *Native Creative Process.* Theytus Books, 1991

- - - *Breath Tracks.*Theytus Books, 1991.

Blesser M. Kimberly.*Gerald Vizenor:Writing in the Oral Traditions,* U of Oklahoma P/Norman Publishing, 1996.

Boaz, Franz et al. *Folk-Tales of the Salishan and Sahaptin Tribes.*Kraus Reprint Co, 1917.

Boal, Augusto. *The Theatre of the Oppressed.* Routledge, 1993.

Boyd, Drick and Chang Heewon, *Spirituality in Higher Education.* Left Coast P, 2011.

Cardinal, Douglas and Jeannette C. Armstrong. *Native Creative Process.* Theytus Books, 1991, pp. 82.

Cameron, Anne. *Daughters of Copper Woman*. Press Gang Publishers, 1981.Colombo, Gary et al. *Frame Work:Culture, Storytelling and College Writing.* Bedford Books, 1997.

Cohen,William Alexander. *School Failed Coyote.* University of British Columbia, 2010. Web 10 July 2018 htttp://open.library.ubc.ca/circle/collections

Damm, Kateri. "Says Who:Conialism, Identity and Defining Indigenous Literature." *Looking at the Words of Our People*: *First Nations Analysis of Literature, edited by* Jeanette C. Armstrong, Theytus Books, 1993.

Denzil, Norman K. *Indians On Display.* Left Coast Press, 2013.

Denzin, Norman K, *Qualitative Inquiry in Neoliberal Times.* Routledge, 2017.

Derickson, Delphine et al. *We Get our Living Like Milk From the Land. Theytus Books*, 1994.

Derickson, Mickey. *Coyote and the Colville.* edited by Yannon/St Mary's Mission, 1925.

Dove, Mourning. *Coyote Stories.* edited by V. McWhorter, Caxton Printers, 1934.

- - - *Mourning Dove (Hu-mis'-hu-ma):A Salishan Auotbiography. edited by* J. Miller. Caxton Printers, 1934.

- - - *Tales of the Okanagan. edited by D.M Hines,* Ye Alleon P, 1976.

Easton, Robert & Peter Namokov. *Native American Architecture.* Oxford UP, 1989. Grant, Catherine. *International Journal of Intangible Heritage.* Volume 5, 2010.

Joseph Sr, Andrew. *The Country of Sen-om-tuse:(sna?amtus)Coville.* Co-published by Andrew Joseph Sr. and Theytus Books, 2013.

Hines, Donald M. *Tales of the Nez Perce.* Ye Galleon P, 1984.

Lane, Phil Jr., et al. *Sacred Tree.* 3rd Edition, Lotus Light, 1989.

Laforme et al., *Reconciliation & The Way Forward.* Aboriginal Healing Foundation, 2014.

Leavy, Patrick. *Handbook of Arts Based Research.* Guilford P, 2017.

Leavy, Patrick. *Research Design.* Guildord P, 2017
Leavy, Patrick. *Art Based Research: Methods Meets Art Based Research Practice.*

Guildford P, 2015.

Luna, James. *James Luna - Emendatio.* P.Smith & T. Lowe (Curators), Smithsonian National Museum of the American Indian, 2005.

Maracle, Lee E. *Isole Nella Corrente Tribalsimo E Ricerca Dell' Identita Nella Cultura Dei Nativa Candesi.* University of Messina, 1992-93.

Martini, Clem. *The Ancient Comedians.* Playwrights Canada P, 2014.

Mathews, Daniel N & Deward E.Walker. *Nez Perce Coyote Tales: The Myth Cycle.* U of Oklahoma, 1998.

Manu Aluli Meyer. *Native Hawaiian Epistemology: Sites of Empowerment and Resistance, Equity & Excellence in Education*, 31:1 (1998), pp. 22-28. DOI:0.1080/1066568980310104.

Morin, Peter. *River Stone.Circle.* University of British Columbia, 2011. Web. 10 July 2018. <https://open.library.ubc.ca/cIRcle/collections/24/items/1.0071711>. Electronic Theses and Dissertations (ETDs) 2008.

Okanagan Tribal Council Elders. *Kou-Skelowh:We Are the People.* Theytus Books, 2004.

Robinson, Harry. *Harry Robinson: Living by Stories.* edited by W.Wickwire, Talon Books, 2005.

Silko, Leslie M. "Leslie Silko's Ceremony:A Laguna Grail Story." *Four American Indian Literacy Masters.* U of Oklahoma Press/Norman Publishng,1982.

Smith Tuhiwai, Linda. *Decolonizing Methodologies: Research and Indigenous Peoples.* Zed Books, 2013.

Smithonsian Institute. *James Luna - Emendatio.* Luna, James;Paul Smith & Truman Lowe (curators) Smithsonian National Museum of the American Indian, 2005.

Vizenor, Gerald, "Beyond the Novel Chippewa Style," *Four American Indian Literacy Masters:Momaday, Welsh, Silko, Vizenor.* U of Oklahoma P/Norman Publishing, 1982, pp.124-148.

Vizenor, Gerald and Blaeser M. Kimberly. *Writing in the Oral Traditions.* U of Oklahoma P:Norman Publishing, 1996.

Velie, Alan D. *Four American Indian Literacy Masters: Momaday, Welsh, Silko, Vizenor.* U of Oklahoma P: Norman Publishing, 1982.

Younging, Gregory. "Publishing In the Margins.*" First Nations Analysis of Literature,* edited by Jeannette C. Armstrong, Theytus Books, 1993, pp.178-188.

Oral Interview

Belanger, Mariel - Co Graduate Student - Oral discussion (telephone), Corinne Derickson July 31, 2018

Derickson, Delphine (mother) Oral Interview, Corinne Derrickson, Westbank, May 10,2018.

Photos

Luna, James. "Artifact Piece" How Luiseno Indian Artist James Luna Resists Cultural Appropriation, JSTOR Daily, Accessed 15 Oct. 2018.

McWhorter Lucullus V. Mourning Dove 1915 V McWhorter Digital Collections Home Content l libraries.wse.edu., Accessed 23 Feb 2018.

Derickson, Corinne, "puta?ntnm i? anxa? cintet" (Honouring our Grandmothers) MFA Project Photo Collection

About The Author

Cori Derickson - Master's of Fine Arts (Interdisciplinary), Bachelors of Fine Arts, Business Admin Diploma, artist and holistic practitioner who recently graduated with a masters graduate degree from University of British Columbia-Okanagan (UBCO) Nov. 2018 lives in Syilx Territory is of Okanagan/Colville/Arrow Lakes -(Plateau), Nez Perce, Hawaiian and Irish descent is a proud mother and grandmother with one great grand nephew.

Cori is a multi-interdisciplinary artist performance major with international experience. Cori traveled to Peru, France and the MidWest USA to share her artistic practice. She is one of the only few female Eagle Dancer's in the world. Her artistic practice include dance, sculpture, painting, photography, music, song, writing, animation and production of multi-media works.

"I have a passion for performance art using the tradition of captikwl (ancient stories). "I come from a family of knowledge keepers and natural storytellers" Cori continues the work of her family through her academics and art including that of her Great Great Grandmother - Mourning Dove - Hemishmish (first Native American published author).

Cori's graduate work includes the research of the traditional performance concepts of theatre based upon the captikwl published by Mourning Dove in "Coyote Stories" (1933-University of Washington State).

"In 2010 I lost my dear son Makwala to a bullriding accident. It was the worst thing imaginable to endure. I turned to the arts as a tool to heal my life. Through art and ceremony I connected to the spirit world to create beauty in artistic ways to share with the world. The practice is comparable to the spitzen (a sacred thread) which connects the physical world to the spiritual world. It is there that I feel comfort close to my Sunshine and the ancestors while continuing my walk here"

MORE FROM EAGLESPEAKER PUBLISHING

AUTHENTICALLY INDIGENOUS NAPI STORIES:
Napi and the Rock
Napi and the Bullberries
Napi and the Wolves
Napi and the Buffalo
Napi and the Chickadees
Napi and the Coyote
Napi and the Elk
Napi and the Gophers
Napi and the Mice
Napi and the Prairie Chickens
Napi and the Bobcat
... and many more Napi tales to come

AUTHENTICALLY INDIGENOUS GRAPHIC NOVELS:
UNeducation: A Residential School Graphic Novel
Napi the Trixster: A Blackfoot Graphic Novel
UNeducation, Vol 2

AUTHENTICALLY INDIGENOUS CALLABORATIONS:
Teeias Goes to a Powwow (a series)
The Secret of the Stars
The Awakening
Young Water Protectors
Hello ... Fruit Basket
Sixties Scoop
... and countless more at eaglespeaker.com

WWW.EAGLESPEAKER.COM

Made in the USA
Lexington, KY
24 November 2019